Red Bus

and

Not in the Bin!

By Rebecca Colby

Illustrated by
Melina Ontiveros

The Letter B

Trace the lower and upper case letter with a finger. Sound out the letter.

Down,
up,
around

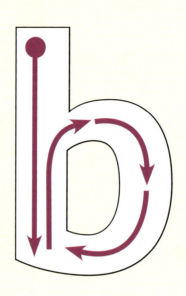

Down,
up,
around,
around

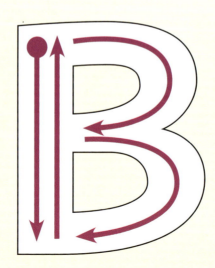

Some words to familiarise:

bus   button   bed

High-frequency words:

on   the   off   go   in

Tips for Reading 'Red Bus'

- Practise the words listed above before reading the story.

- If the reader struggles with any of the other words, ask them to look for sounds they know in the word. Encourage them to sound out the words and help them read the words if necessary.

- After reading the story, ask the reader to name somewhere the family visited.

Fun Activity

Try drawing a red bus!

Red Bus

Get on the red bus.

Hit the button.

Riiing!

Get off the red bus.

Go in.

Go back on the red bus.

Hit the button.

Get off the red bus.

Sit on the red bus.

Hit the button.

Hotel

Get in bed.

The Letter I

Trace the lower and upper case letter with a finger. Sound out the letter.

Down,
lift,
dot

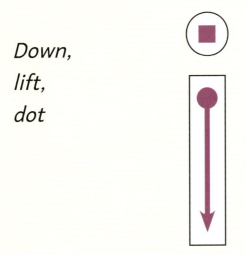

Down,
lift,
across,
lift,
across

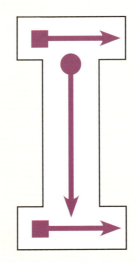

Some words to familiarise:

bin   sock   rag

High-frequency words:

in   the   put   on   it   is   a

Tips for Reading 'Not in the Bin!'

- Practise the words listed above before reading the story.

- If the reader struggles with any of the other words, ask them to look for sounds they know in the word. Encourage them to sound out the words and help them read the words if necessary.

- After reading the story, ask the reader what the boy made.

Fun Activity

Make something out of recycled materials!

Dad put the sock on the mat.

Not in the bin!

Dad put the buttons on the mat.

Dad put the rag on the mat.

Dad put the lid on top.

29

Book Bands for Guided Reading

The Institute of Education book banding system is a scale of colours that reflects the various levels of reading difficulty. The bands are assigned by taking into account the content, the language style, the layout and phonics. Word, phrase and sentence level work is also taken into consideration.

Maverick Early Readers are a bright, attractive range of books covering the pink to white bands. All of these books have been book banded for guided reading to the industry standard and edited by a leading educational consultant.

Pink

Red

Yellow

Blue

Green

Orange

Turquoise

Purple

Gold

White

To view the whole Maverick Readers scheme, visit our website at www.maverickearlyreaders.com

Or scan the QR code above to view our scheme instantly!